MW00456356

The Collective Unconscious.
By Amro Ali

Amro Ali

Copyright © 2019, The Collective Unconscious by Amro Ali.

All rights reserved. No part of this publication may be reproduced, distributed, or transmitted in any form by any means, including photocopying, recording, or other electronic methods without the prior written permission of the author, except in the case of brief quotations embodied in reviews and certain other noncommercial uses permitted by copyright law. For permission requests, contact: amrowrites@gmail.com.

Cover art and all illustrations by Fatima Batool.

ISBN 978-1-7054-1890-1 (paperback)

Amro Ali

CONTENTS

Amro Ali

For my parents, who have shown me God and life and everything that lies in between. May Allah forgive me if I have wronged you.

Amro Ali

Jubair bin Mut'im reported: I heard the Prophet, peace and blessings be upon him, reciting *Surat al-Tur* in the evening prayer. When the Prophet reached this verse, 'Were they created by nothing? Or were they themselves the creators? Or did they create the heavens and the earth? Rather, they are not certain! Or do they own the treasures of your Lord? Or have they been given the authority?' (52:35-37),

I felt my heart was about to fly.

{Ṣaḥīḥ al-Bukhārī 4573}

Amro Ali

EVANESCENCE.

Amro Ali

how do i speak of today?
here, i watch my father bear dirt
and saltwater down my throat.
i have never been cleaner,
or whiter.

i sit studiously through the burial,
i have already prepared my
answers for *munkar* and *nakir*.

i keep their memory alive in a
pocketbook under my skin.
i thumb through it when death
feels close.

-    *if tomorrow were death day*

it was the coldest summer, i believe // your home was a carriage drawn by ~~my~~ our mother's rawboned arms // her only guiding light the spittle gathered on your bottom lip // the white wet snow that fell in june // before your arrival all we had was a pile of what would've been ~~my~~ our brother on the kitchen island in a glass tupperware container // ~~my~~ our mother was meat for the butchers // her beloved falling from between her legs like a heavyweight // like feces // like something dirty destined for toilets and drainage pipes // i reckon had he been brought in a carriage like you he'd be just as beautiful and brown // the same thick lashes and gap toothed smile // the same curly hair and rebellious personality // had this earth been a prayer mat i'd hurriedly press my forehead to his tiny gravestone in our backyard five times a day // images of his silhouette in our fridge playing like a kinetoscope behind my eyelids // the stars twinkling above our heads like a canopy of minarets // i'd pray for his gapped teeth // for his brown skin // for his hair // praying and praying until i remember the backyard grass has dog piss all over it and that unborn babies are guaranteed heaven;

only then do i remember to pray for you.

only then do i remember to pray for myself.

-   *on my sister's birth*

first born daughters are

        landfills for weariness

they're shoes worn thin

        for eighteen years with

the big toe peeking out

        the front to see what all

the ruckus is

        they're hair falling out

and deep pools of cold

        sour lemonade under the

eyes everyone loves

        drinking from

        [*especially the kids*]

these trees are papier-mâché
folded origami style by bandits
who dream only to tear my skin
to shreds when i need it most.
this grass? *sandpaper*. grinding
foot to dust from the heels up,
uprooting heaven from soles
that never felt baby fingers grip
their toes, never played peek a
boo in ocean water or tasted
africa in their footsteps.

this is
a gentrified being, a compass
needle carrying on its face names
it does not know how to pronounce.

- *identity crisis*

everything is hard

for she whose limbs are butter

sweet salt on bone melting

away like the meat she is

if only words danced on her

like blade did

would her poetry be any

more profound?

\-   *the butcher 's specimen*

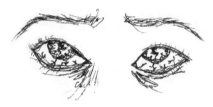

I am told to keep quiet till I heal. It seems I am destined to be silenced indefinitely.

-       *If I bleed will you hear it fall?*

I've never been too fond of opening up. My father always seems
frustrated by this fact, clawing at his scalp until he remembers that stress
withered his hair away, staring at the mess I've made of myself with eyes
that beg for answers I don't know how to give. It's this occurrence that
hurts the most. Yesterday he asked me why I never seem to be happy
with anything in life, in this same fashion, his hands scratching his head
as if to reminisce what was once there, the hair he used to take pride in,
his eyes fixated on the war taking place on my left forearm. My teeth
dug deep into my tongue, my esophagus tangling itself like two
wrestlers on a blood-stained mat, words and wind fighting to the death.
And I never know how to untangle this knot, explain this mess, wipe my
father's eyes, ease his tension, speak. Ironic, coming from me, the self-
proclaimed poet who supposedly knew how to make words bend metal,
how to make song out of nothing. If only I could make song out of my
being, out of the limpness my body succumbs to, the head that spits acid,
the mind that melts to chow, the ears blood pours out of; out of the heart
that beats silently, the prayers I whisper through gritted teeth, the tears
that pool into clasped hands; out of the pain I existentially feel, the way I
want it to end, the means I take to end it; out of the hurt I bear to others,
the witch I've somehow become, the curses invisibly etched into my
forehead; if only.

And yet, through it all, my father stays and listens to the silence I have to give. My lips clamp shut and he listens with his eyes, reading whatever story is written on my face that day, whatever story the paintings on my arm present themselves to be. You were the only one who showed me what patience was, father, and every day I take your lessons for granted, brushing them aside like the night sky brushes aside the sun. Every day I forget that you are the Sun, in every aspect of it, that I am born to represent everything dark, the moons reincarnation. I'm sorry for attempting to coexist with you; God knows light and darkness were never fashioned to mix, never born to share the same sky. So I will settle with the dirt, as I am nothing, and to nothingness I am destined to return.

The sky is all yours, father; teach it love as you have taught me.

-   *a suicide note, for whenever*

Amro Ali

REMINSCENCE.

Amro Ali

in front of his house the moon sits
on the porch & exhales stars onto
every crack in the graying cement
sweat coated cousins sing hymns
with cicadas the loudest on fridays
his papyrus skin is a vessel carrying
seven years of imprisonment &
decades more of africa on its back

when i was younger i would pine for
stories of *sovietica* & the taste of
war in springtime & instead i was
met with bedtime songs about flying on
his thumbs as a baby & never once
smelling death on their tips

is it the metal, *awoowe*?
or is it God, that taught
you how to make things fly?

-    *grand · fa · ther*

she had eight holes in

total on each ear

& cancer was a tiny mole on

her breast

motherhood ripped nine

tears in her belly

& she accepted each

one with a wince

every day she asks her lover

        do you know what lies beyond the red sea?

& everyday he says no

but winces too.

dementia took everything

from her

except how after seventeen years

of languish a man

arrived with a pistol on

his hip & offered

gold from his canines

as dowry for the pearl of the

indian ocean

my uncle was born with an

inevitable

soldiers' gait & told his mother

stories of life beyond
 what moses touched with
his staff
& for once she grinned from
earring to

      earring to

          earring to

      earring to

earring to-
seventy-three years later
her daughter's
daughter sits in a bedroom
encased in
languish writing
about how she wishes
she could find love in the
land of the
lions too

   -   *of gold & musk*

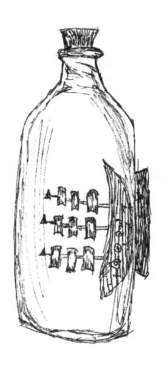

five times a day
uncle's voice is a milky
white minaret &
virginia becomes mecca

Glory be to God!

the pavement kisses his
forehead like a brother &
the chesapeake finds home
in his tears

- *blind man taught me 2 read*

you showed me God once.

    placed me on your shoulders

    at the beach so i could stand on

    them & see how far the earth stretched

He held me in the balance. you

& Him. the sky & the earth

& i was what was in between.

      a photograph of you is

      on our fridge, smiling, all your

      teeth visible except the front two

now, all your teeth are visible

except the front two. manhood

sits in the door jamb, beckoning.

    you do not look at it.

        death sleeps in your left pocket.

    its metal is heavier than me.

your shoulders feel my feet again.

this time, a hole is in the ground.

    the sky & the earth

& you are what is in between.

-   *if gun violence should claim u, cousin*

the ticks of the clock have grown
deafening, mother.
my ears ring with it, loudly,
keep me up at night.

the wind whistles & *tsk-tsks* at
my state through the window, my
nose buried in a book i yearn to
tell you about, as i used to.

you'd be half-listening, half-
thumbing through the cupboard
above the oven, raining flakes of
cardamom & thyme on the kitchen
island, greasing your palms with
refined black seed oil.

do you hear it?
the clock? it mocks me, mother.

the pen leaps from my fingers
& scribbles something onto
my school notebook.

it is not the answer.

will you speak to me
today, mother?

will the clock stop
for a minute,
just for a second, i promise
& bring me your voice?

      -   *i am hoarse from the*
          silence

The stab of diffidence is still there, gnawing, redirected. The wind blows seasons in and years by; it blows me along with it too. Grandmother is old now. She forgets things. Smacks me on the head for not saying *salaam*. I kiss her forehead and say *salaam* for the ninth time that day. My grandfather speaks only of death and masks anticipation with laughs that carry a whistle - I can hear the clock ticking between his ribs. War is painted behind his eyelids. He counts his brothers' bodies on his fingers. My cousin counts them on his neck. I count mine in my palms. Sometimes my eyes are gray. My sister asks what I daydream of. Her patience wears thinner than water. I tell her the sky looks like a painting today. *It's just clouds.* Father sees it too, the pink and blue. The yellow. The water. Mother tastes rain before we do. Brother is blind again. Does he hear it? The thunder? Grandfather says a prayer. *It's just clouds.*

I hope so too, for our sake.

- *how to heal*

yesterday has blood

    drying on its floors

the room smells like

    metal & bitter things

& when bodies are

    mixed in the ground

becomes a pulpy mess

    strung together by hairs

of my brothers & sisters

    i pick out my teeth with

yellow bones handed to me

    with a smile and a wink

colors that smear it dulling

    with rot & voices that

sang lullabies once now

    muted faces that shone

like sun once now dimmed

    hearts that swelled with

the words of their Lord

    once now bone-thin

& their ashes just as

    parchment-paper white

   -   *the dead aren't dead till you forget*

from my bedroom i hear my mother
drop a dish & weep
it is 6pm & the dinner table is still
naked as it was this morning
i fold a pillow over my ears
& try to fall asleep amidst the shattering

my baby sister bounds into my room
& nestles beneath my arm warm
& soft until i feel her snores vibrating on
my skin & hot urine racing down her leg
i groan & shout from the stairs that
i cannot bear to smell it another second

my mother's hands are overworked even
when she is not cooking or cleaning up
our waste she is fingering the line that
cut her belly open & remembering the
pain that tattooed her eyelids red

when she looks at me too long i
wonder if she is remembering a time
when i was not a reminder of happier
times but an embodiment of them

she tells me she is tired of me taking her
things without her permission &

i do not know how to tell her
i fear a day when i will open her drawers
& face my selfishness square in the face
instead of her perfume

-    *how do i repay the years i owe you,* hooyo? *i have been unfaithful.*

Amro Ali

DEHISCENCE.

Amro Ali

i am told i am a sea of clay // femininity weeps in the dip where the chieftains stole my hips, their marks lying on my frame like scythes on wooden lovers // if catharsis was a man he would lay here too, unscathed, all empyrean curtain drawn over saturn's bosoms and a coat shadowing the celestial embodiment of ineptitude // & ~~she~~ i am *woman* // a veil draped across her teeth and still her smile shines brighter than hell // i've begun to notice they only ever hang the lonely ones // if dark things are evil then loneliness must be periwinkle blue, but less romantic, & womanhood as red as childbirth // all i have to do is dream to tell the universe to take good care of my baby // god knows we need all the prayers we can catch on our eyelashes // doomsday is right around the corner of our bedrooms // my pen scratches its surface every now & then // i can taste it whenever womanhood knocks on my door & bleeds.

- *womanhood is scarlet*

if only my poems

weren't strung thin

like saddle leather

papyrus i'd tie

your words together

with septum rings and

summer air to

bend at your waist and

draw... hook... toss!

i'd finally dip my toes

in your lake water

hoping you'll learn

the hard way to catch

me when i fall

-     *sometimes fishing reminds me of you*

1

spicy green chili and sore thumbs
stuck in between gapped teeth
bellies full of cornmeal chai tea mustaches
and bumps and bruises still healing
from wood spatulas thrown skillfully
at the head i never duck fast enough

2

running hands along new body i
never knew was there this whole time
discovering what a woman is, *you ARE*
what a woman is, you. *me?*
i peak at the mirror again with shy
eyes that kiss the floor more than anything

3

thick black eyelashes and soft eyelids
glued shut fingers pressed on lips *you*
can't wail here because the neighbors
will hear you mouth crooked because
it doesn't know whether to say *i'm sorry*
or drink up tears from carpet

4

i've learnt what it means to have هيا

zipped lips and burnt jeans in the

trashcan the cul-de-sac smells like a crime

scene manila folder shut for good like

eighteen years of dust blown off in one huff

i tie the fabric with ease now

5

the mirror cocks its head to the side

as i stand in front of it calculating if

i'm woman enough to have eyes pretty as

two chocolate drops peeking through slit

ripped in fabric i see my mother come up

behind me claws bared tear new skin from my

face the scar she leaves is pink and

pulsing it has a face too

6

and all that remains of me forever *woman*

are my eyes.

- *ode to the reflection i see, and all the ugly things*

I. this existential crisis is marked by longing // sometimes i hear
    my pen erupt in a rage and wish i could match its energy //
    sometimes i gather myself and belt *thank god for poetry! // thank god*
    for the poets! // sometimes i thank god for men and the muses they
    bring // very often i lose sight of my womanhood in the smoke
    of teenage angst // i am not woman *enough* // i am not fit to be
    something seductive yet // to have the sun laid naked on my skin
    and to bathe in grass and drink kombucha // right now i'm
    woman enough for green tea and bullet journaling, i think;

II. other times love doesn't make it past the front gates of my teeth
    // if i still had a gap i would like to think you'd get stuck there,
    in those gates // sometimes my desires manifest themselves in
    bankai form // days when my hands bleed tragedies kin to no
    other, in calligraphy // the pen winces, i wince, the paper laps it
    up // this is routine // this is poetry for the dogs // sap for those
    who have long since died from thirst;

III.   and still i write // in hopes that one day a coffee shop (not starbucks, too cliché) will have a poem of mine (not this one, *please*) push pinned to a cork board somewhere in the back // behind the bathrooms and the trash cans // and someone will stop by and feel something other than lactose intolerance and the shits.

-    *do people still go to poetry readings?*

my words won't find a home here
my pen isn't a vessel for prayers too
quiet to be heard past the drip of its ink
doesn't bend at the knees legs crossed
in the dark and paper origami folded
towards the sky; they don't feel safe
not here with drunk men bellies filled
to the brim so high you can see whiskey
sloshing around in their mouths his skin
smells like gunpowder and rope burns
hands calloused from gripping death for so long

you can smell it too

especially when he tries grabbing your chin
to say how pretty you are
you spend days looking for your face in
glass books you flip through and it shows
on every inch of your sinewy arms
the blood that colors you red like *bindis*
and *tandoori* powder turning brown as it
marinates on skin and sticks there bright as a
scar you'll try spitting at to wipe clean like mom did
everything reminds you of mom nowadays

even the orange of the sky at sundown that
looks like the *diraac* she used to wear
when she cared about looking pretty for daddy
the one that brought the sun to its knees at every
doorstep split every uterus into two halves
one for Man and one for the Sun
and from each bore forth two sons

one wilting in her womb before it could
taste this air that isn't meant for beautiful
black boys with skin of gold and honey
and if she should have to hold her dead
child
between her knees barely formed
just a heap of meat with a heartbeat and a
smile I swear I see behind my eyelids
every night by God I pray it be the one
from the Sun

{for of the two I swear he is the strangest}
-   *glad tidings*

There is a voice in the back of my head that tells me I'll never find love. Not like in the movies. I am five-foot ten flat footed, six-foot three in heels, a question mark of a woman - both physically and metaphorically, my hunchback being one of many things I have grown to be more conscious of the more my mother calls it out. My lower gut, another. I watch Humphrey Bogart and Shah Rukh Khan movies at night hoping I'll see love as bold and true in someone's eyes as the heroines do. How can I, though? The wind does not sing my name, nor does the earth lay flat for me to run through its grass and into my hero's arms. I only know twilight hour buzzcuts I try to convince myself were necessary for psychological growth, not long brown tresses that smell of flowers and rain. There was no Parisian swan-like transformation for me; I am the same girl I was five years ago, ten even - the only differences being I have two new holes in my nose, a haphazard afro, and I look like my mother if she liked indie things. She doesn't. My room is a mess. I can't see the sun anymore. My bed holds me and makes everything feel better till I can't feel anything at all. Then the sun arrives, or as much left of her as we can see. There are mere months left until I am a foreshadowing of THE twenties.

I am expected to be a woman by then. Every poem (or essay, or whatever) in this book thus far has discussed womanhood as a question mark. A question mark? Womanhood! As it is. My body is expected to stretch for a man and his seed, to extend all parts of me to welcome the storm that is capital-m Man. With a silent grimace. With grace and hips wide enough to carry life in them. I am not *hayaa'* less. I can keep my mouth shut and accept what God has ordained for me (after all, fighting against decree has never done me well) and I shall accept this too. I shall swaddle and allow myself to be suckled. I shall continue to vigorously pray I get to taste romance in places other than Frank Sinatra songs and black and white movies before the aunties begin to whisper that I've expired, like milk or other awful things. Will I shrivel if I am unmarried by (*god forbid*) twenty-five? Or, (I can practically hear the aunties having heart attacks in unison here) thirty? Are all my years of education and building for naught, then, if not tied off with a pretty bow at the prime of my life by a man? As a writer, it is in my description to crave love for writing material, and half of my *deen*, but little else. I am a romantic. A hopeless (and hapless) one. A too-tall, too-insecure, but- with-standards-far-too-high-to-be-realistic one.

And that is okay.

How funny would it be, if my Humphrey Bogart were reading this right now? If so, I beg, Casablanca awaits, and so do the aunties. Arrive soon, for my sake.

- *Casablanca, or Autumn Leaves (whichever you prefer)*

Amro Ali

LUMINESENSCE.

Amro Ali

I am as whole as I am meant to be right now.
I am whole

and I am loved.

-     *mantra*

There are days
when I miss the simplicity
of seeing my parents kiss and thinking
it was the most repulsive thing in the world.
How incredibly tragic that the funeral
downstairs is a vat of gasoline that does not
know how to burn off on its own - the
women have tea-stained teeth and bellies
too and I am so so so swollen with
children that are learning the hard way
to claw a path out of my throat.
The taste of a rotting woman is a delicacy
of the most delicate sort.
When I am especially curious and
hurting I discover Pangea is dying between
my legs before I can ask my mother what the red
stuff is. The barrel of my pen is as dark as
that of a shotgun but I find solace in it anyway.
There is no poetic way, I've found, to say I
am afraid of men, of being touched, of what the
lamp on my bedside table looks like when
it is off and my door is folded in on itself.
Has Israfil done it, I hear, or is it his breath
on the horn? I cower.
What is poetry if not an objection of
the world and everything
born from it?

Let us start from the origin.
What spell has been cast on me
that I have been deemed a poet?

I alert my mother that this does not look like
Springfield anymore. Where is our townhome?
What a glory, to find myself in a city I have
yet to write myself into. My hair hasn't been
in pigtails since I was five and lovable.

And no, I did not once ask God for immortality.

- *I am afraid of everything but especially myself*

the suburbs @ five am in july is;
teeth. limp tongues and sharp canines
drilling cubbies inch deep down windpipes
choked raw with voices stifled for as long as
they've known how to speak. this is fishhooks
dug into knuckle beds like marionette clasps,
fishlines tearing bodies through the sky like
rag dolls that never bothered to digest the
concept of animacy. this is the sun ripped
naked from her chamber and laid bare on her
back showering life beneath her feet in naked
heat, the moon peeking at her breasts with
shy eyes through lashes braided thick with
twinkling stars and shame; she's comfortable.
and warm. everything blushes and
blossoms as the sky turns pink.
as do i.

i am a butterfly at every mention of your name

    fluttering until every part of me vibrates

    like one single note a hummingbird

    never gets tired of singing

    for you

    for nikki giovanni

    who wrote a love so pure

    the kisses still lingered on your hands

    after a good read

i am a poem at every mention of your name

the pen leaps and forgets its purpose

at every stroke i still never tire of writing

    for you

   for whatever my words mean to you

   if i were to pool in your lap

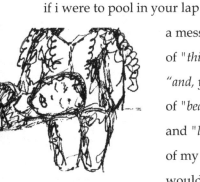

    a mess of flesh and fire

    of *"this one's for you, tupac shakur!"*

    "and, yeah, this is a love poem"

    of *"beautiful black men"*

    and *"love is-"*

    of my simple declaration of love

    would my skeleton still sing

     for you?

i've wandered through

this souk countless times

in the weeks that i was here

a man sells me *bakhour*

& asks for my hand in

marriage at fourteen

i've never in my life

seen more light than

the silver that beams off

his nine encased teeth

the beasts treasured rose

lies there, in his mouth

i tell him how frankfurt

carried me to the house of

god on its snow white

wings an animal that is

more ribs than feline

kisses our toes & i let it

as i sleep spiders build

caves in my nostrils & till

now i have never tasted air

so whole

    -   *medinah;* المدينة المنورة

The nurse at the doctor's office saw my arm today as she drew blood and said nothing of it. We discussed mundane, cheerful things, the weather, for example, and how cold my hands felt in hers. I silently awaited the inevitable moment when the world would implode on itself, when she noticed the stripes that marked my arm from the bend of my elbow to the top of my wrist, for my heart to fall out my mouth and lie still in front of her and the rest of the hospital staff, but, instead, we made small talk. Small talk. We talked about her kids and the sports they play, what she planned on making for dinner that night - my arm sat there, attentive, quieter than usual, an afterthought. An afterthought.

An afterthought.

- *Is this what reclamation feels like? Like a lump in your throat?*
I kind of like it.

growth is a process like watching spaghetti water boil over right next to the *uunsi* rock bellowing smoke on the stove. i should know because the whole house smells like salt and sandalwood and chipping ceramic and it is the best and worst time to have guests over. when i stretch my arms out they crackle and pop and in that moment i am more tumbleweed than feminine. it is easy to forget that the dandelions in our yard are overgrown sometimes. i sit nestled in my friends' comradeship until the seat warmer isn't the warmest thing in the car. it's us and it's being alive right here right now in this car alive and breathing. laughing until we pee and laughing at us peeing and laughing at how one day we'll be so old we'll feel fuzzy inside when we tell our children we once laughed so hard we peed. getting lost in department stores with no other purpose but to dance through the aisles and sniff the mothball repellents and swear that i have never inhaled anything more beautiful. except *uunsi*. except salt and spaghetti water.

once, on a whim, i purchased a ten ninety nine ridiculously massive fraying floppy hat that i later realized i have no intention of wearing outside the confines of my bedroom. it sits perched on my mirror and collects dust but it is okay because the women i know are just as vast as any beach. my sister, for example, is a new woman, all taffy limbs and awkward body but she is adjusting to the growth nicely. she is more beautiful than me, and i do not need to swallow my pride to admit it.

my mouth is just about the haughtiest thing about me, but if poetry must be a means for something then it is a means of declaring ones love and this is even more than that; this is a manifestation of adoration. beyond blood we are tied together by our womanhood.

albeit perplexing, my sister, you are a woman and it has been divine, to say the least, watching you cocoon.

my other sisters, although not kin, are written in my palms just the same. we are back in the car again and we are singing our hearts out and bopping like no one is watching even though we know they are but if we care it sure as hell is not written on our faces. despite coming from two poles of the world it is remarkable how we are different shades of the same brown. i see them in me. we talk of bangladesh and somalia and ethiopia and mecca and medinah and our tongues twinge with reminiscence but we are not emotional because we don't know how to be. we've never tasted white sand and all the camel jerky is month-old and imported but we love it anyhow. and with a start i break the silence and *so which one of us do you think is going to get married first?* we all know the answer but we don't at the same time and we are anxious. our understanding of the unknown is finite and blissful and i do not know if we will ever be okay with it.

why do i look at the sky and see so much that i cannot comprehend? because i am not really looking. like how i believe 'selfish' is a curse word. like how i cannot grasp that doing things for the self is not an unholy deed, no matter how much poetry write.

when i was in middle school, the first poem i ever recreationally wrote was titled *l'oubliette*. i took french for eight years and knew enough to know l'oubliette meant 'the forgotten place,' or simply a pretty way of saying dungeon. i can't remember what it was a metaphor for. now, i could write about a million and a half oubliettes (my body, for example, or how love is something i cannot wrap around myself when it is cold out.)

l'oubliette also knows my arm is the most crippling thing for me to remember. i live with it's presence blindly, avoiding its existence at all costs. the doctor asks me to roll my left sleeve up for routine blood work and i decline as calmly as possible and leave. this is routine, too. i have stopped counting how long i've been clean. the last time i salivated at the idea of hurting myself was november something. today i googled the cost of skin grafting surgery and cried. there are not enough poems in this world i could sell to gather enough money to rip the skin clean off my arm and make a hundred scars disappear. the despair that comes with hating a limb is not something i can explain in writing so i will not try. despair isn't even the word. there is no word for limb-hatred.

maybe i need therapy. or maybe i need laser surgery. or maybe i need to press my stomach to the asphalt and count to ten and when i open my eyes there will be my answer standing in front of me, on the sidewalk, and it won't be blasphemous but as God-sent as anything i've ever touched.

and so we run until we find a bend in bed bath and beyond secluded enough for us to take pictures in that i can stare at until they become ugly, and even then we are so entrancing and if i could i would print them all out and tape them up on every inch and corner of my bedroom wall because our happiness is beaming off of our faces and i have never loved us more than in that moment. even when we are ugly we are in love with each other and our company and i do not know a purer feeling than that, to be loved even when you feel you are anything but deserving.

i have never given myself time to grow. that is because i have only ever had time for self-loathing and pain. my mom bought me mederma advanced gel scar treatment a few months ago, a fifteen dollar treatment with a promising title and slow results. i used it once and watched it bubble and peel. the next morning, the scars were still there, present and brown as ever. mederma stares at me from the medicine cupboard when i go to take my vitamins. i do not stare back.

and while on the topic of beaches, my mother is a woman above all living others. her spine is a curved watering hole but i know from the decaying snapshots that decorate our fireplace mantel that there was once a time when she was regal and stood taller than everyone else and when i look at myself with my shoulders bent inwards i can see the woman she was. i have inherited everything and more from her. when the facade falters so does the air and i struggle to breathe. who knew giving life takes so much of it out of you?

how many kids do you want to have when you grow up? but first i yearn for a day when lido beach is not a story in photographs for me, when i can see the blue-green shoreline my mother raced towards on her way home from italian school and i can let her footsteps fall through my fingers. for when i can see the church ruins and the house she grew up in and the bullet hammered walls and shingled roofs and hear the *adhan* in the streets. maybe when i can point to a map and tell my children *this, here, this long snaking coast, this is where your grandmother grew up and it was the most beautiful place, i saw it for myself* then i will have a numerical value to place on how much of myself i am willing to suck out with a vacuum.

when the unknown is the conscious. when i can look at the bricks and the bricks look at me and i can hear the stories the kiln couldn't melt away.

if i am honest i am afraid of a lot of things but i am most afraid that my roots will become so fragile that the only thing i can associate with myself is the fact that i exist.

what do you to say to that? nothing at all.

all i know is that every day that i am here i am loved and i am not entirely there but i am brimming with things that i am grateful for and that is enough to anchor me until my toes can't taste my soul anymore.

even if this is the last time that i will ever write a word i am grateful for the stories i have told and the ones i have listened to with my legs crossed and with tears brewing in my belly and the ability to brandish a pen and make it do something meaningful.

even if this is the worst thing you have ever read in your life at least you are reading it and it is registering something in you.

even if this is the last time that we will dance through the parking lots of the world to the music of nothing but the universe grinding against itself i am glad that i have done it with love radiating off of my skin and smiles engulfing every bit of me.

and on the days that i forget what that feels like, i will read this and remember the smell of the sandalwood and the salt and the love and the growth and if i am selfish for that then so be it.

let it be known that i am the most selfish woman to have ever existed for loving myself and for loving the act of receiving love.

is there anything more human than that?

- letter to;

Amro Ali

It is my condition to heal. I pray that, one day, my bones will become accustomed to the pangs of growth.

Amro Ali

Amro Ali

Amro Ali

Acknowledgments;

Where do I begin? Thank you so much to everyone who has had a hand in making this book possible. This journey could not have been possible without your valuable input. Thank you to Fatima, for your artistry and for being an absolute dream to work with. You brought my writing to life in ways I never knew was possible. I will forever cherish the artwork you created for this book. Thank you to my ~~best friends~~ ~~sisters~~ two out of the three stooges, Yasmin and Sumaita, for being my makeshift editors and for thumbing through every inch of this book with me for weeks on end, for soothing my anxiety, for reminding me of my purpose. Thank you for always believing in me, for always being there to make me laugh when all I knew were tears. Thank you to my family; I do not need a reason to thank you other than the simple fact that you are there and have always been. Above all other worldly things, thank you to my parents. I cannot express in words how grateful I am for your lessons, for your faith in me, for your love and how you've raised me. All good things I am are from the both of you. Thank you for always being in my corner and believing in me before anyone else did, and especially when I didn't. I love you.

All praise is due to the Most High.

And to the readers, thank you for choosing to be apart of this journey with me. I cannot thank you enough for your time.

Amro Ali

The Collective Unconscious

Made in the USA
Middletown, DE
11 January 2020

82815855R00046